THE VOICE OF AN ANGEL

Inspired Writings
By
Sandra J Yearman

SERAPHIM PUBLISHING LLC

WE WILL BRING LIGHT TO ALL THE DARK PLACES

Registered trademark-
Sandra J Yearman
Seraphim Publishing
438 Water St. Cambridge, WI 53523

Copyright © 2008 Sandra J Yearman
Produced in the United States of America
Author : Sandra J Yearman
Editor: Sandra J Yearman
Cover Design by Sandra J Yearman
Layout and design by Sandra J Yearman

All rights reserved. No part of this book may be reproduced, stored in or introduced into a retrieval system, or transmitted, in any form or by any means, electronic or mechanical, including photocopying or recording or otherwise copied for public or private use—other than for "fair use" as brief quotations embodied in articles and reviews--without written permission from the author.

Library of Congress Control Number: 2009906921
ISBN: 978-0-9815791-8-4
First Edition

God Inspire Us And Help Us
To Overcome
The Images In Our Minds
That Block Our Holy Sight
Amen
Amen
Amen

CONTENTS

DEDICATION

An Angel's Voice.................................7
His Presence I Should Know..............9
Souls Ignite......................................12
God Bless Your Helpers...................14
The Shepherd 16
False Gods.......................................18
Light..20
Fall From Grace...............................22
As Angels Hover Over 23
Let Me Soar.....................................26
God Is Always With Us...................28

SEEKING LIGHT IN THE DARKNESS

In His Hands He Will Cradle...........31
Why Would We Blame God............34
Lost Souls..37
A Single Tear...................................38
Seeking the Truth............................40
Crossroads.......................................42

CONTENTS

Angels With Broken Wings..........................44
Forgiveness...46
Tortured Souls...48
Humanity..50

COMING HOME

The Voice Of An Angel................................53
Journey With A Friend................................55
A Single Feather Falls 57
Peace Of God..59
Grace..60
The World Bows...61
Dream Weaver..63
Seeking Light In The Darkness.....................66
The Dance Of The Immortals 68
I Am Who You Seek......................................71
The Lord Is At Hand.....................................73
Life's Lessons..75
Call Upon Angels..81

Dedication

An Angel's Voice

The Angels in their glory
Stand before; I am told
All of God's creations
To protect from satan's hold

With their Holy Mercy
They cleanse away our tears
They heal us and protect us
And conquer all our fears

God in all His wisdom
Blessed us with these friends
Who watch and listen to us
Who Love us without end

In their arms they carry
With their wings unfold
They defeated all darkness
And broke the devil's hold

Never will they leave us
Never are we alone
For God's plans are perfect
For He will bring us Home

Amen Amen Amen

His Presence I Should Know

I saw a purple Angel in a dream
His Holiness aglow
He said that God had sent him
And his presence I should know

His color was God's Majesty
His wings God's Holiness
He cried the tears of Heaven
At humanity's frailness

He talked to me of Heaven
And God's Love, without end
He told me of Forgiveness
And the gifts God gives to men

'We see you as God's children'
'We see you as God's gifts'
'We Love you without boundaries'
'And from darkness, we would lift'

He asked me why we would not listen
He asked me why we would not see
That nothing in this human world
Was hidden from the Trinity

'All your thoughts and actions'
'And motivations; please'
'Are known by all of Heaven'
'As well as all your deeds'

'God keeps sending you His manna'
'And His words for all to read'
'Yet, to follow in God's footsteps'
'You fail to see the need'

'To see the Face of Heaven'
'To bring the monsters down'
'For Faith and Forgiveness'
'Are the Holy Crown'

And as he asked these questions
He showed me as he sees
A world of darkened chaos
A world of war and greed

But I could not find an answer
Because I do not understand
Why we could have the Grace of Heaven
And choose the fall of man

Amen Amen Amen

Souls Ignite

Doves
Daybreak
Light eternal
Messengers from Heaven

Spiraling upwards
Flight of the soul
Dance of the ancients

Distance worlds
Stars ignite
Souls up-lifted

Chains are broken
Doves

God send us Your Holy Light
Save us
Lift us from this darkness
Bring us Home

Amen Amen Amen

God Bless Your Helpers

God bless those who are the eyes
Those who are the ears
And those who are the voices

God bless those
Who save
Who carry
Who heal

God bless those
Who stand before
Who teach
Who do Your Will

God bless
Their love
Their compassion
Their courage

God bless the Angels among us

Amen Amen Amen

The Shepherd

Jesus
The Son of God
The Salvation of this world
The Song of Heaven

Came to us in the image of man
That we might understand

Came to us in our own image
To calm our fears

Led the life of a human
To teach us by example

He taught us
He fed us
He healed us

He took our death sentences

So that we would not have to suffer the tortures of hell
For we are not innocent

The Song was not silenced by the darkness
The prisoners were set free
The world was not sentenced to death

Because our Savior stood before us
Because our Redeemer showed us that we could conquer death
Because with His resurrection He gave us life

Jesus
Make us worthy to be Your children
Make us worthy of Your Sacrifice
Forgive us and heal us
Help us to conquer death

Amen Amen Amen

False Gods

Lord protect us from those who would disguise themselves as righteous

Lord save us from those who would pretend to be holy teachers

Lord stand before us when darkness projects false images of light

Lord expose the false gods and false prophets

What a victory for darkness when it steals the flock from the shepherd

Lord, You are our Shepherd
Our Truth
Our Way
Our Light

Lord guide us and show us the path of Righteousness

Lord carry us and help us to stay on Your path

Lord Forgive us

Amen Amen Amen

Light

People have not really changed since
Biblical times
We still have the same strengths and
weaknesses
We still have the same fears and
desires

We have advanced but have we evolved
As civilizations
As groups
Or as individuals

Can one star brighten the night sky
Can one candle illuminate the
darkness
Can one spirit bring God's Light into
a darkened world

Please God Bless me that I may be
A star
A candle
An instrument of Thy Will

Bless me Lord and help me to bring
Your Light to all the dark places

Amen Amen Amen

Fall From Grace

Even the righteous can fall from Grace
If they do not ask God to carry them

Even those who appear to be holy
Can be conquered by darkness
If they do not ask God to walk with
them always

Even those who walk in the light
Can be darkened by sin
If they do no ask God to dwell in their
hearts

God never leave us
Lord never fail us
Heavenly Father carry us always
And stand before us

Amen Amen Amen

As Angels Hover Over

As Angels hover over
Waiting for us to pray
To ask them to help us
And in our lives to stay

As Angels hover over
And 'speak to us' they say
To carry and protect us
To show us God's Holy Way

As Angels hover over
A tear they sometimes cry
Because we do not listen
And choose a path to die

As Angels hover over
Their presence we fear
We do not want to believe
That Holiness is near

As Angels hover over
And Bless us every day
And show us Love and Mercy
And in our lives they stay

As Angels hover over
Their presence represents
The Love that God has for us
A Love that's Heaven sent

In their wings we cradle
In their Love we heal
In their Holy Presence
To our Holy God we should kneel

Our choices they destroy us
Our fears are in control
The darkness we call defeats us
We are in danger of losing our souls

Yet God, His Love He shows us
His Mercy without end
Our sins He Forgives us
And His Angels He does send

Amen Amen Amen

Let Me Soar

Lord let me feel Your Presence
Help me to understand
Help my eyes to see
Let my heart be uplifted

Lord help me to hear Your Song
Consume me with the melody of
Heaven
Teach me the ancient dances
Give me the voice to sing songs long
forgotten

Lord carry me that I may be cradled in
Your arms
Lord steady me when I stand against
darkness

Lord prepare me for the walk down
the paths of life
Lord give me wings that I may soar
above this dark world

Amen Amen Amen

God Is Always With Us

God is always with us
He is not some unattainable being
He is not some distant perception

He is real
He is here
He is All

His image is distorted by men's agendas and motivations

His image is belittled by those who would compete with Him for power and glory

His image is defiled by those who justify darkness by using His Name and His words

God help us to understand Your Word and Your Will
God help us to find You among the distorted images

God show us what is real
God Bless us with Your Presence
God let us hear Your Voice

Amen Amen Amen

Seeking Light In The Darkness

In His Hands He Will Cradle

I was already dead
I had not yet lain my body down
When I heard the Song of Heaven
And the chaos it did drown

Angels came before me
Their blessings they gave
They changed my life forever
And my soul they did save

They showed me life worth living
Alone I would never be
They loved and they blessed
And promised forever to be with me

Love transcends all boundaries
All worlds and even more
Love can heal all darkness
And allow this world to soar

God is Love
He creates all that lives
The wonder and the beauty
And His Holiness He gives

Life can seem crazy
By the chaos we create
By the choices, by the actions
And the mistakes that we make

No matter what our journey
No matter how dark our way
As long as we have faith
We will overcome, He did say

Talk to God, they told me
Pray and you will see
That God listens and He answers
And in His Hands He will cradle thee

Amen Amen Amen

Why Would We Blame God

The doors are closed
Abandoned
Lost

Fear
Guilt
Spiraling into darkness

God are You punishing me
God this is Your fault
Consumed with anger

The choices are ours to make
If we choose to shut our doors to God
If we choose to reject His Spirit
If we choose to walk in darkness

How then, does God enter

Does He force His way through the closed door

Does He take away our freedom of choice

Why would we blame God for the results of our own thoughts and actions

Why would we be angry at God
When we never let Him in

God cleanse the darkness from us
God heal us that we may understand
God forgive us and save us

God teach us to walk in Your Light
God consume us with Your Spirit
God teach us to pray

God help us to let You in

Amen Amen Amen

Lost Souls

Lost souls
Floating between existences
Searching for their home
Floundering
Ever winding
Ever seeking
Endless trails
Confusion
Nothing seems right
Nothing appears as it is
Illusions

Please Lord, help those who have lost their way
Find Your Holy Light
Find their way Home

Amen Amen Amen

Single Tear

As I look around me
I see need

I hear the cries
Of anguish and terror

We are becoming numb
To the horror we create

We summon the darkness
And feed it with our fears

Jesus wept for us
And the Angels cry

A single tear from Heaven
Could cleanse and save us
If we would choose to
Allow God's Will to be done

God walk with us in these dark worlds
Your Presence is needed here

Amen Amen Amen

Seeking The Truth

Bless the seekers
Bless those who would brave the
darkest of places
To carry the Light of God

Bless those who thirst
With the Living Water

Bless those who hunger
With the Living Bread

Bless the warriors, the healers,
The teachers and the shepherds

Bless us with Your Mercy
Heavenly Father
Bless us that we may find

Your Truth
Your Light
Your Way

Bless us with Your Holiness
And forgive us our sins

Amen Amen Amen

Crossroads

When the pain will not stop
The wounds will not heal
And the darkness is endless

When you are tired of existence
When you are in the middle of a crossroads
And every choice is filled with pain

Pray
Pray
Pray

God will listen when no one else will
God cares when no one else seems to
God is there when the world betrays you

Ask God
To carry you
To heal you
To help you make the right choices

Ask God to help you live again

Amen Amen Amen

Angels With Broken Wings

The packaging is different
The container is broken
The vessel is the wrong color

We label
We categorize
We discriminate

We hate
We neglect
We discard

We are all God's children
God is Love

If God Loves His creations
Why don't we
Why don't we
Why don't we

God help us to see Your creations as
You do
God help us to Love as You do
God help us to see past

The fear
The hatred
The labels

And see the Holiness in all of Your creations

Amen Amen Amen

Forgiveness

We dwell in the past
We remember the anguish
We re-live the pain

We feed the anger
We empower the jealousies
We cradle the revenge

We allow hatred, mistrust and fear
To grow within us as malignancies

These malignancies
Consume
Control
Destroy
Our spirits

Often our past prevents us from going forward
Often our past destroys our present
Often our past imprisons us

Heavenly Father forgive us and teach us to forgive
Heavenly Father cleanse the darkness from us
Heavenly Father help us to heal
Heavenly Father help us to let go of yesterday and to live again

Amen Amen Amen

Tortured Souls

When the horror and the terror
Are so overwhelming
That identities are lost
That spirits are murdered
That souls are fractured

When the victims exist without living
When cries are without sound
When souls are lost
When the darkness is impermeable

When pain is the only sign of life
When time ceases
When the warriors are crushed
When the tears come no more

Lord God,
Help those who can not speak
Help those without voices
Help the victims

Lord God,
Please heal us and save us
Please Bless us
Please restore our souls

Amen Amen Amen

Humanity

We project our fears and guilt onto others
We blame
We hate

We segregate
We torture
We murder

We justify our unholy motivations and actions
By accusing others of wearing the masks of our demons

Oh Merciful God, please forgive us

Oh Loving God, please save us from darkness and death

Oh Savior, please bring Your children Home

Amen Amen Amen

Coming Home

The Voice Of An Angel

Would you use your voice to change this world

Would you stand up
Would you stand before
Would you stand at all

Would you face the abyss
Would you face the darkness
Would you face your own soul

Would you risk
Would you carry
Would you bless

God carry me that I may do
Your Holy Will

God hold me up to the face of
Darkness

That we may bring Light to this dying
world

God Bless me that I may not falter

God give me a voice that I may help to
bring Your children Home

God fill me with Your Grace and keep
me on Your Holy path

Amen Amen Amen

Journey With A Friend

You demanded to see the Face of God
I asked to wash His feet

You cried to Heaven to awaken
I asked to be His tool

You were proud of your accomplishments
I asked to be given the words

You asked for wealth beyond your means
I asked to be given me what I need

Ask God to help you understand
And you will realize He is sending you the answers

Ask God to help you overcome
The images that block your Holy Sight

All the paths are the same
The journeys are unique

Amen Amen Amen

A Single Feather Falls

Taking flight
Wings wavering
My soul leaves my body
Speeding through time
Speeding through galaxies

Searching for the ancient truths
Soaring
Timeless
Teacher

And a single feather falls

Jesus teach us the timeless truths
Help us to understand
Teach us to do Thy Will

Jesus carry us in these worlds
Forgive us
Bring us Home

Amen Amen Amen

Peace Of God

Life without chaos
Life without pain
Life without loneliness

Life without terror
Life without anguish
Life without fear

Imagine a life where the only
Tears you cry are tears of
Joy and Holiness

Heavenly Father
Send us Your Peace
Fill us with Your Presence
Heal us from the nightmares we have created

Amen Amen Amen

Grace

Healing
Joy
Holiness
Amazing
Completeness
Love without limits
Eternal
Radiance
Peace

God Bless us and fill us
With Your Grace

Amen Amen Amen

This World Bows

This world bows
To wealth
To images
To false power

This world glorifies
Horror
Might
Monsters

This world ignores
The children
The victims
The cries

This world is weighed down by darkness
This world is destroying itself
This world...

Lord please reach through these
illusions of hell
And bring us into Your Holy Light

Lord please remove the obstacles from
our hearts and souls
That we may remember that we bow
To no one
To no thing
To no illusion

But the Majesty and Glory of our
Heavenly Father

Amen Amen Amen

Dream Weaver

Illusions
Worlds
Nightmares

Life is the thread in the tapestry
Our choices each strand
Our strands entwine

With all others to form
The paths
The designs
The destinies

God's Holy tapestries
The art of the Heavens
The foundations of the worlds

Our paths
Our choices
Our faith

God of all creation, bless us and help us to see the tapestry

Help us to understand that God is life
And that we dwell in a living tapestry

Help us to understand that every life
Is woven and represented in this tapestry

Help us to understand that every choice, every action is a strand in the grand design

God forgive us
Give us the faith and the strength
To allow You to guide and direct our choices
In Your Holy tapestry of life

Amen Amen Amen

Seeking Light In The Darkness

We must seek to find
We must question before we can
receive answers
We must remove the obstacles from
our eyes
Before we can see

Holy One, keep me on a Holy path
That I may seek Your Truths
That I may understand Your Will
That I may hear Your Voice

Help me to always know and to do
Your Will
To the best of my abilities

Holy One,
I seek the ancient truths
I ask to hear the ancient Song
I want to dance the ancient dance

Holy One, Bless me and use me as
A tool of Your Will
An instrument of Your Peace

Amen Amen Amen

The Dance Of The Immortals

Lord help us to remember the dance
of the immortals
Our dance, before our fall from Grace
Our dance of faith in Spirit
A dance that transcends all time and
space

Lord help us to let go of the fears that
constrict us
We are immobilized by our sins
Our hatred and un-forgiveness
Creates the prisons that we are in

Lord help us to hear the Song of Heaven
To free us from our chains
To surrender to Your Spirit
And immortality to gain

Let Your Spirit dwell within us
And guide us in this dance
That we surrender to Your music
And sing the Holy chants

The Spirit will control us
And to Heaven we will soar
The unholy darkness
Will imprison us no more

The dance of the immortals
To the ancient songs of old
Bring the Peace and Grace of Heaven
And its Holiness unfold

Darkness will never triumph
Darkness has no chance
To deter me from my Savior
Or to stop this Holy dance

Amen Amen Amen

I Am Who You Seek

As I lay dying
My spirit burdened and meek
I called out to my Lord
His Holy Face to seek

And in my dying hour
A Voice I heard speak
'My child, my child'
'I AM who you seek'

I felt my body quiver
I felt my body shake
My tears were flowing
I was cleansed of my hate

When my legs would hold me
I stood up from my bed
My body filled with strength
I no longer walked among the dead

I turned my face to Heaven
And through tears, I cried
Forgive me Lord
I will always walk at Your side

My life was changed forever
The moment I heard God's Voice speak
I soar among the living
God's Face I will always seek

Amen Amen Amen

The Lord Is At Hand

He is in
He is of
He is all

His Presence
His Love
His Grace

Is accessible
Everywhere
Every moment
To every being

Just pray
Just say

Lord I choose to walk in Your Holy Light

Lord please forgive me, my sins

Lord replace the darkness within me with Your Peace, with Your Grace, with Your Majesty

Amen Amen Amen

Life's Lessons

In my hour of darkness, I met a man of light
Our meeting was God's message to me; a lesson I learned well
For this holy encounter
Brought me out of my self imposed hell

His body was disfigured
His enormous head on his shoulder had to rest
His fingers braced with metal
Not to stare, I did my best

His body was immobile
A chair provided legs
The lesson that he taught me
Has stayed with me all these days

A mirror, he held before me
In it, my darkness I did see
The image that I saw
I did not recognize as me

He sat across the table
With his physical frailties
And when he bowed his head and prayed
I realized, I was the one with the deformities

He thanked the Lord for his blessings
He was grateful for his life
He asked God to bless others
And to help them through their strife

As my tears were flowing
He turned to me to say
'do you believe in God'
'I speak with Him every day'

The image in that Holy mirror
My demons it did show
God dissolved them in His Holy Light
And the lessons I still know

Perception is a gift from God
A power in its right
For we can choose to sink in darkness
Or to walk in God's Holy Light

My life it is a blessing
And every occurrence is Heaven sent
For there are no chance encounters
Every moment it is meant

To allow us to make choices
To give us opportunities
To define our inner being
To become the person we will be

This young man he did show me
That I had gone a stray
My anger and my hatred
Were filling all my days

I prayed to God through eyes of tears
For forgiveness and that He
Would heal me and restore me
And His Holy Light to see

And this time I asked God to carry me
And to never let me go
For the demons I saw in that mirror
I never again want to know

Because in my self pity
And the anger that filled me
I was sinking into darkness
My blessings I failed to see

As the years have traveled
And as my life has changed
I ask God to help me make Holy choices
And my life to arrange

The answer was so simple
But I fought it with such might
I chose to leave the darkness
And to walk in God's Holy Light

Amen Amen Amen

Call Upon Angels

Let Angels walk in these halls
Let Angels walk in these fields
Let them live in our homes
Let them act as our shields

Let Angels sit at our tables
Let Angels join in our feasts
Let them sing the songs of Heaven
Let them stand before the beast

Let the Holy messengers of Heaven
Be known to all creation
Let them be called upon
By every man in every nation

Let there be no place so dark
Let there be no place so filled with fear
That creation forgets
They can call the Angels near

Call upon them
In song and in praise
Call upon them in prayer
To accompany you all your days

Let the word 'Angel'
Be comfort and friend
In every language and land
For time without end

Amen Amen Amen

God Send Us Your Holy Light
Save Us
Lift Us From This Darkness
Bring Us Home
Amen
Amen
Amen

www.ingramcontent.com/pod-product-compliance
Lightning Source LLC
Chambersburg PA
CBHW051711040426
42446CB00008B/822